MW00437467

Learning to Play the Game

by Adam McClellan
illustrated by Dan Grant

PEARSON

Scott
Foresman

Editorial Offices: Glenview, Illinois • Parsippany, New Jersey • New York, New York
Sales Offices: Needham, Massachusetts • Duluth, Georgia • Glenview, Illinois
Coppell, Texas • Ontario, California • Mesa, Arizona

Every effort has been made to secure permission and provide appropriate credit for photographic material. The publisher deeply regrets any omission and pledges to correct errors called to its attention in subsequent editions.

Unless otherwise acknowledged, all photographs are the property of Scott Foresman, a division of Pearson Education.

Photo locators denoted as follows: Top (T), Center (C), Bottom (B), Left (L), Right (R), Background (Bkgd)

Illustrations by Dan Grant

24 Phil Schermeister/Corbis

ISBN: 0-328-13547-X

Copyright © Pearson Education, Inc.

All Rights Reserved. Printed in the United States of America. This publication is protected by Copyright, and permission should be obtained from the publisher prior to any prohibited reproduction, storage in a retrieval system, or transmission in any form by any means, electronic, mechanical, photocopying, recording, or likewise. For information regarding permission(s), write to: Permissions Department, Scott Foresman, 1900 East Lake Avenue, Glenview, Illinois 60025.

4 5 6 7 8 9 10 V0G1 14 13 12 11 10 09 08 07 06

Creeaak...slam! Every time the moving truck went over the tiniest bump in the road, it would shake and shudder, making a racket like an old screen door slamming shut. Ella didn't mind. From the passenger's seat high above the ground, she watched her new neighborhood pass by.

Although Ella didn't mind, her twin brother Pete did. Pete, who was sitting in the back seat with Ella, groaned, "Oof . . . I don't feel so good."

"Almost there," Dad said, looking at the street signs for the right turn. "Hang on for just a bit longer."

"I'm not kidding," Pete said, "I feel really bad. This truck is making my stomach hurt."

Now Dad groaned. "Come on, Pete. We're almost there." But Pete kept groaning, so Dad pulled over and put on the brakes. "Ella, will you walk your little brother the rest of the way? Just follow the street to number 2729."

Ella sighed. "Fine, I'll walk him." She opened her door, unbuckled herself, and hopped out onto the sidewalk. "C'mon, Petey," she said.

"I'm not some kind of family pet, you know. I can walk on my own," Pete said as he slid out of the truck.

Ella slammed the door shut. "Are you sure? It doesn't look like it from what I can see."

"You just watch," Pete muttered as they began walking up the street toward their new home.

Ella didn't answer. She heard a car rumble up behind them and honk twice. Mom waved as she drove past them in their station wagon, loaded down with stuff.

They were moving on to the newest street in the neighborhood. Out beyond their street, the land was vacant, with only some scattered trees, patches of grass, and a few signs advertising where new neighborhoods were going to be built. Half the houses they passed weren't even finished yet. Ella could see the spaces where windows and doors would go.

For a second, she wondered if she and Pete would arrive at their new house only to find out that it wasn't done, either. Ella imagined spending the first night sleeping without a roof over her head. *Ugh*, she thought to herself. *That would be the worst!*

Ella breathed a sigh of relief, though, when she got to the house with her brother. It was definitely finished! The house was bright blue with a red door, and there were windows that reflected the sunlight. Mom and Dad were already carrying boxes out of the back of the truck and into the house.

"Okay, you two," Dad said. "Go ahead and get a drink of water from inside the house. Then you can start taking in stuff from the car. Peter, is your stomach OK now?"

"It was better as soon as I got out of the truck," Peter replied with a big smile on his face.

"Good to hear," Dad replied. "Then let's get going!"

The twins went inside. "I think the kitchen's this way," Pete said, his voice echoing through the empty house.

Ella followed her brother into the kitchen. On the counter were two plastic cups full of water that Dad had filled for them. Ella handed one cup to Pete. She gulped the other one down.

"It's a big place," Pete said.

"Empty, too," Ella said. "Let's go get our stuff."

For the rest of the afternoon, Pete and Ella helped their parents haul boxes into the house. There was so much that had to be moved! Beds, furniture, clothes, appliances, towels, linens, silverware, and more all had to be brought in to the new house.

By nightfall, Ella and Peter were exhausted. They both went to their new bedrooms and instantly fell asleep.

The next morning was a Saturday. Pete asked Dad, "When are we taking the truck back?"

"We'll return it this afternoon," Dad said. "Until then, you've got the whole morning to do whatever you want. Why don't you guys head over to that park on the corner. You know, the one we drove by yesterday. I think it was called Hippershill or something."

"Whippoorwill," Ella corrected. "Well, why not? Want to come, Pete?"

"Sure," Pete replied.

After breakfast, Ella and Pete headed down to the park. There were lots of kids there, all talking in a group. The talk died away as soon as the kids saw Ella and Pete approaching.

"Hi," said Ella. The sudden silence made her nervous. "Ummm…we just moved in. I'm Ella, and this is my brother, Pete. Pete, say hello to everyone."

"Ummm, hello?" was all Pete could say. Ella could tell that her brother was as nervous as she was!

A tall girl with blond hair nodded. "OK, Ella and Pete," she said. "I'm Tiffany. We're going to play Two Bases. Want to play?"

"Sure," Ella nodded. "Is it like baseball?"

Tiffany shook her head. "I'll explain after we pick teams. Ray and I are captains. I pick first today." Tiffany then pointed to a short boy in a red shirt, making him the first player to be picked. Ella was chosen ninth, and Pete was taken last. He marched over to Ray's side, frowning over having been picked last.

Tiffany's base

Tiffany pulled her team together and explained the game to Ella. "Each team has a base. Ours is this tower, and theirs is that bench over there. Each team has two taggers. You and I will be taggers for our team, and Ray will be one of the taggers for their team. If a tagger tags you, you go and stand at the other team's base. When one team captures all the other team's players, that team wins."

Ella nodded.

"There's a ball, too," Tiffany added. "Anyone can pick it up and throw it at a player on the other team. If anyone gets hit with the ball, they get sent to the other team's base. But if you catch a ball that's thrown at you, you're safe, and you can then throw it at a player on the other team."

"Got it," Ella said. The rules didn't seem too complex.

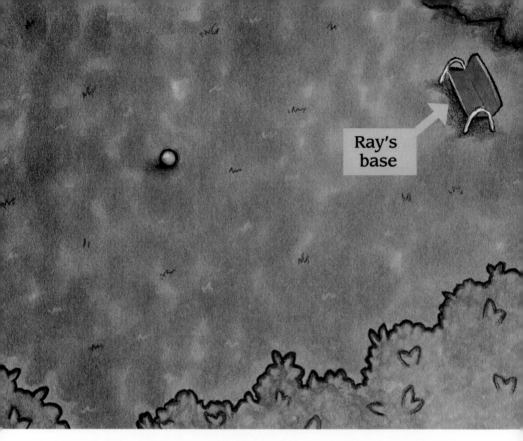

Ray's base

The game started with a race to the ball, which lay in the middle of the playground. Ray reached it first. He threw it at Ella, who ducked. Behind her, someone scooped it up and started chasing Pete. Ella turned and ran back to her teams' base. Before long, Tiffany showed up with someone she'd caught.

"Who's the other tiger on Ray's team?" Ella asked her.

"The other what?" Tiffany asked. "Did you say tiger?"

"Of course I said tiger," Ella shot back.

Tiffany burst out laughing.

"What's so funny?" Ella asked.

"It's *tagger*, not tiger!" Tiffany said, still laughing. "As in someone who tags something."

"Oh," Ella said, blushing.

"Anyway, the other team's tagger is Navin. He's the one in the football shirt," Tiffany added.

The game was moving quickly. Tiffany captured another kid from Ray's team, and Ella caught Pete. Only three people were left.

Out of the corner of her eye, Ella saw the ball roll past her. She moved toward it, but suddenly noticed a boy in a blue shirt with the number 32 on it running straight for her. It was Navin! She turned and ran for her base as quickly as she could, barely touching it before Navin did.

Something wasn't right, though. The captured players from Ray's team were cheering and high-fiving. Then they started walking back toward the other side of the playground.

"Ella! What are you doing?" Tiffany hollered.

"I got here first!" Ella shouted. "Pete, get back here!"

Tiffany ran over. "Navin touched our base! He set all of his captured teammates free! Why didn't you tag him?"

"What are you talking about?" Ella cried.

"I told you that Navin's one of their taggers. If a tagger touches the other team's base before you can tag him, then the tagger gets all of his captured teammates back!" Tiffany shouted.

"You didn't tell me that!" Ella shot back.

"I told you to watch out for him!" Tiffany stormed off.

For the rest of the game, Ella was too upset to think straight. Ray tagged her, she was set free, and then she was hit with the ball and sent back to Ray's base. From there, she sat and looked on as her teammates were captured one by one.

Ray's team cheered as the game ended. Ella watched with envy and turned to Tiffany. "Are we playing again?"

"No," Tiffany said, looking away from her. "Not today. Maybe Monday after school." Tiffany got up and brushed off her pants. "I'm going home for lunch."

"Fine!" Ella called after her, still upset over everything that had happened.

Pete wandered over to his sister, and together they began the walk home.

"Man, I got tagged three times," Pete complained while they walked.

"Hmmph," Ella complained. "At least your team won."

The following Monday was Ella and Pete's first day at their new school. The school, like the rest of the neighborhood, had been built recently. But the other students acted as if they'd been there for years. They knew what was being signaled when the teacher flicked the lights on and off. They understood which school bells meant what when they rang. And they knew where the cafeteria was and how the locks on their lockers worked.

Ella didn't know any of those things. She felt embarrassed and confused.

Ella passed Pete once in the hall. He didn't seem happy about his first day either.

Ella hoped things would improve after school, but they didn't. On the playground, Ella was picked for Ray's Two Bases team, just ahead of Pete.

When the game started, Ella ran for the ball, but Tiffany got there first. As Ella was fleeing back to her base, she felt the ball bounce off her leg. Ray got caught trying to free her, and after that the game was as good as over.

That night, Ella confronted her parents.

"I hate it here," she announced.

"Why?" Mom asked, her newspaper rustling as she laid it on the coffee table.

"Everyone at school ignores me. I've tried playing this game that all the other kids play, but I'm no good at it and I hate it." Behind her, she heard Pete's footsteps.

"Yeah," he said. "I can't stand this place, either."

"Come here," Mom said. She took Peter and Ella's hands into hers and rubbed them gently. "It'll get better."

"It will definitely get better," Dad said from across the room. "After all, it's not as if we've moved to a new country or a different civilization," he said. "It's just that the other kids have been here a few months longer than you. But you two will do fine, just as you always have."

"And, Ella," Mom said, "making a few blunders in some game isn't a big deal. You'll get the hang of that too."

By the end of the week, Ella began to think that maybe her parents were right. At school, she seemed to be getting the hang of things. Ella had learned that when the teacher flicked the lights, it meant "everybody quiet." She had figured out the way to the cafeteria and learned which school bell meant what. Even better, two new kids had come into her class. Ella felt better knowing that she and Pete were no longer the only new kids.

Still, things could have been a lot better. It rained on Wednesday and Thursday, so nobody played Two Bases. Both days, Ella sat on the bus listening to the kids from her neighborhood making plans to play at each other's houses. But no one invited her and Pete over to play.

Friday afternoon was warm and sunny. Ella and Pete ran to the jungle gym just as the other kids were picking sides.

"Hey, it's Ella and her little brother," Navin called out. "How are you going to make your team lose this time, Ella?" Navin laughed.

Ella ignored him and thought hard. Navin's teasing had inspired her to come up with a plan. But would it work?

Tiffany picked Ella and Pete last for her team. As she gathered them all around, Ella said, "Hey, I've got an idea."

"Who cares about your idea?" said Tiffany. "Let's play!"

The game started differently this time, as Ray's team had a new strategy. They won the race for the ball, but instead of charging after the weaker players like Pete and Ella, they ran around on their side of the playground, passing the ball back and forth.

All of a sudden, Ray took the ball and threw it toward
Ella, Tiffany, and the others, high into the air. Tiffany
jumped to make the catch, but it went over her head. Out
of nowhere, one of Ray's teammates ran in, scooped up the
ball, and bounced it off Tiffany's back. Then the ball rolled
over to Pete, who picked it up.

Cheers erupted from Ray's team. Ella groaned. They
were down to just one tagger already. From what Ella had
seen, the first team to lose a tagger usually lost the game.

Ella called her teammates together while Tiffany was
being taken over to Ray's base. "We have no choice," she
said to her remaining teammates. "We have to try my plan!"
Ella gathered them into a huddle and began whispering.
Their eyes grew wide with excitement as Ella explained. It
sounded like the plan could work!

When the game started again, Ella ran straight out into the middle of the field.

"Navin!" she called out. "You think you're fast? You're not. All you are is lucky!"

Ella stood there with her hands on her hips, waiting to see what would happen.

Navin didn't say a word. Instead, he grinned and started running straight for Ella. Ray and the rest of the team followed right behind.

Ella turned and began fleeing as fast as she could toward the jungle gym. *So far, so good,* she thought to herself.

Ella checked behind her. Navin was gaining, but he was still more than ten feet away. They were getting close to the jungle gym now. Ella turned one more time and slowed down a bit. *Here goes nothing*, she thought. Ella made herself bump into one of the corner poles, and then fell down as if she had been stunned.

"Oh, this is too easy!" Navin crowed. Slowing down, he walked up to tag her.

"Now!" Ella suddenly shouted. Pete jumped out from beneath the jungle gym, where earlier he had hidden with the ball. His throw got Navin in the side. Navin stood staring at Pete with his mouth open. In the meantime, the ball bounced to Ella, who jumped up and flung it at Ray. He attempted to catch it . . . but the ball spun off his hands and onto the ground.

"Yeah!" Ella's teammates began shouting as they ran up to her and Pete to give them high-fives.

"Nice toss, Pete. You got both of them!" Ella said as she patted her brother on the back.

Pete was embarrassed by the attention. Still, he was able to crack a smile. "I couldn't have made the nice toss if it wasn't for your nice plan."

"Way to go, Ella!" Tiffany cheered from the other side of the playground.

Ella grinned and waved. Their team was back in the game! *Maybe Mom and Dad were right after all*, Ella thought to herself. *Things are getting better. Now if I could just figure out how to free Tiffany!* Ella raced back to the action, happy to be playing the game.

Town Festivals

Moving to a new city or town can be challenging. One great way to get to know your new community is by attending a local festival or celebration. The following harvest festivals are famous throughout the country.

The town of Warrens, Wisconsin, is called "The Cranberry Capital of Wisconsin." Up to 100,000 visitors attend its yearly cranberry festival. People celebrate by making cranberry pie, cranberry salads, and even cranberry chicken!

People who want something sweeter can head to Opelousas, Louisiana, for the "Louisiana Sweet Potato Festival Yambilee." Each fall Opelousas celebrates the end of the harvest with a weekend of feasting and entertainment.

And for a crunchier snack, head west to Yuma, Arizona. "Yuma Lettuce Days" celebrates the city's most important crop with jugglers, country music, and a "Salad Toss-Off."

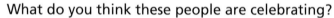

What do you think these people are celebrating?